GOLDFISH

MICHAELA MILLER

Contents

Words in bold, **like this**, are explained in the glossary on page 23.

Goldfish

All the goldfish in the world are descended from a fish called a wild Crucian carp. These goldfish were first kept as pets by the Chinese over 1000 years ago. Goldfish were first brought to Britain just over 200 years ago.

common goldfish

Today, there are lots of different kinds of goldfish. They are all related to each other.

GOLDFISH FACT

Goldfish like to be with other goldfish. It is unkind to keep one goldfish by itself.

3

The goldfish for you

Comets, shubunkins, fantails, goggle-eyed — these are all types of goldfish. But common goldfish are better for beginners because they are stronger and may live longer. Other types can be more difficult to look after.

comet tail goldfish

GOLDFISH FACT

A goldfish longer than 12 cm really needs to live in a pond.

Common goldfish are often sold at garden centres and pet shops. You can also look for the names of **fish dealers** in your local newspaper.

shubunkin

Home sweet home

Before you bring any fish home, you will need a proper tank and equipment. You can buy this from a pet store or **aquarist** shop. It can be quite expensive and complicated, so go with an adult.

Fish tank equipment should include a **filter** and an air pump. The tank also needs a cover to stop the fish jumping out, a good layer of gravel on the bottom, some smooth rounded rocks, water plants and some **fluorescent tube lights**.

healthy goldfish

GOLDFISH FACT

Fish can easily get too hot or too cold in tanks kept on window ledges.

Buying your goldfish

Your goldfish should come from somewhere that is clean and well looked after. The tanks in which the fish are swimming should have clear water and lots of room.

buying a fish tank

GOLDFISH FACT

Fish gulping at the water's surface might not be getting enough oxygen.

Goldfish are sometimes given away as prizes at fairgrounds or fêtes. Do not get a goldfish here. These fish may be very unhealthy. Sometimes they die before their owners get them home.

9

Healthy goldfish

Any goldfish you choose should have a well-rounded stomach and bright, clear eyes. There should be no cuts, growths or parasites on their scales or fins. Drooping, lifeless fins means the fish are not well.

Fish swimming on their sides, lurking in the background or lying on the bottom of the tank are probably not very well either. A thin brown line coming from the fish's bottom is a sign of **constipation**.

This goldfish has a swollen body. It is unwell.

How to handle goldfish

Fish can get hurt quite easily. They do not like sudden changes in temperature and light. **Vibrations** upset them too, so do not tap the tank with your fingers.

a fish net

GOLDFISH FACT

A goldfish bowl is too small for fish. It lets in too much light and not enough oxygen.

Never touch a fish with your hands. Your hands seem soft, but they are not soft to a fish. They can damage the fish's delicate surface. When you have to move your fish, catch it gently with a smooth net. Then carefully put it into another container with the same water and light as its home tank.

Keeping clean

You need to replace up to one-fifth of the tank's water every two to three weeks. You should also take away any dirt from the gravel. The new water should be **dechlorinated** and the same temperature as the water you have taken out.

taking out some of the tank water

Sometimes the sides of the tank become green. You can buy a scraper from a pet shop to clean this off. Clean the wool or foam in your **filter** by rinsing it in **aquarium** water. You will need to get new wool or foam if it is very dirty.

washing the filter

Feeding time

Buy special goldfish food from a good pet shop and follow the instructions carefully. You should take away any uneaten food after ten minutes. A feeding ring, which you can also buy from pet shops, makes the job easier.

feeding ring

GOLDFISH FACT

Too much food in the water makes it dirty and may even kill the fish.

You can also feed goldfish a little chopped lettuce, spinach and oats. This will stop them getting **constipated**.

Ask the expert

It is very difficult to take a sick fish to the vet. It is a good idea to find a local vet who knows about fish before there are any problems.

If you look after your goldfish in the way this book tells you, they should be very healthy for many years. Your goldfish may be so happy and healthy that they start to lay eggs.

GOLDFISH FACT

A well looked after common goldfish could live for 25 or even 30 years.

Eggs and young fish

Goldfish eggs are tiny, the size of pinheads, and sticky. The female spreads the eggs about and they usually stick to plants.

GOLDFISH FACT

Young fish are called fry.

Adult fish often eat the eggs and the young fish. To hatch some eggs, you will need another tank with the same water and temperature conditions as your first tank. Move some eggs and the plants they are fixed to into this tank. The eggs will hatch out in four to fourteen days.

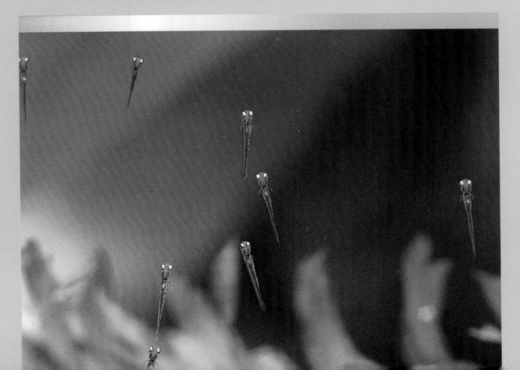

21

A note from the RSPCA

Pets are lots of fun and can end up being our best friends. These animal friends need very special treatment – plenty of kindness, a good home, the right food and lots of attention.

This book helps you to understand what your pet needs. It also shows you how you can play an important part in looking after your pet. But the adults in your family must be in overall charge of any family pet. This means that they should get advice from a vet and read about how to give your pet the best care.

Why not become a member of the RSPCA's Animal Action Club. You'll receive a membership card, badge, stickers and magazine. To find out how to join, write to RSPCA Animal Action Club, Causeway, Horsham, West Sussex RH12 1HG.

 FURTHER READING

Walking the Goldfish by Michael Hardcastle

Glossary

air pump   helps to keep **oxygen** in the water

aquarium   a tank or pond in which you can keep live fish

aquarist   someone who knows about fish kept in tanks, and who can give advice about fish care

constipated   when a fish can't go to the toilet

dechlorinated   tap water with its chlorine taken out. Chlorine is put in tap water to kills germs, but it can make your fish ill. So before putting tap water in your tank, let it stand in a bucket for 24 hours. Pet shops also sell tablets which will take away the chlorine.

disinfectants   used to clean floors, kitchens and bathrooms. They kill germs, but can be poisonous and kill fish.

filter   this helps to keep the water in the tank clean

fish dealers   people who breed and sell fish for money

fluorescent tube light   these are lights which don't make the water hot. They also last a long time.

oxygen   is in the air we breathe. We need it to live, and so do fish.

vibrations   movements in the tank or the water. They happen when people move or hit the tank.

Index

First published in Great Britain by Heinemann Library, Halley Court, Jordan Hill, Oxford OX2 8EJ, a division of Reed Educational and Professional Publishing Ltd

OXFORD FLORENCE PRAGUE MADRID ATHENS MELBOURNE AUCKLAND KUALA LUMPUR SINGAPORE TOKYO IBADAN NAIROBI KAMPALA JOHANNESBURG GABORONE PORTSMOUTH NH CHICAGO MEXICO CITY SAO PAULO

© RSPCA 1997

Designed by Nicki Wise and Lisa Nutt

Illustrations by Michael Strand

Colour reproduction by Colourpath, London

Printed and bound in Italy by LEGO SpA

01 00 99 98 97

10 9 8 7 6 5 4 3 2 1

ISBN 0 431 03366 8

British Library Cataloguing in Publication Data

Miller, Michaela

Goldfish. - (Pets)

1.Goldfish - Juvenile literature

I .Title II . Royal Society for the Prevention of Cruelty to Animals

639.3'7484

Acknowledgements

The Publishers would like to thank the following for permission to reproduce photographs:

Dave Bradford pp6, 7, 17; Trevor Clifford p9; Max Gibbs p15; Photomax pp2, 3, 5, 8, 10-14, 16, 19-21; RSPCA p18 Tim Sambrook

Cover photographs reproduced with permission of : RSPCA; Dave Bradford

Our thanks to Ann Head and her pets; Pippa Bush, Bill Swan and Jim Philips for their help in the preparation of this book; Pets Mart for the kind loan of equipment; Lucia (p17).

Every effort has been made to contact copyright holders of any material reproduced in this book. Any omissions will be rectified in subsequent printings if notice is given to the Publisher.